I turned away
and she was gone

A play | JENNIE REZNEK

I turned away
and she was gone

A play | JENNIE REZNEK

Published in 2019 by Modjaji Books

Cape Town, South Africa

www.modjajibooks.co.za

© Jennie Reznek

Jennie Reznek has asserted her right to be
identified as the author of this work.

Edited by Elaine Davie

Cover text and artwork by Monique Cleghorn

Cover photograph by Mark Wessels

Book layout by Andy Thesen

Set in Legacy

Photography by Mark Wessels on pages iv, 10, 16, 19, 21,
23, 27, 32, 43, 46, 55 and 59, and by Jesse Kate Kramer on
pages 1, 3, 7, 14, 17, 33, 41 and 48.

Printed and bound by Print on Demand, Cape Town

ISBN print: 978-1-928215-70-7

ISBN ebook: 978-1-928215-71-4

To my mother, Rose.
And to Zac and Hannah-Rose.

Credits

Written and performed by Jennie Reznek
Directed by Mark Fleishman
Choreographed by Ina Wichterich
Original music by Neo Muyanga
Set design by Craig Leo
Lighting design by Mark Fleishman

Stage History

2014: First Performed at Magnet Theatre, Cape Town.
2015: Hilton Arts Festival, KwaZulu-Natal; Magnet Theatre, Cape Town.
2016: Magnet Theatre, Cape Town; The Market Theatre, Johannesburg; Frascati Theatre, Amsterdam, Netherlands.
2017: Hellwach Theatre Festival, Hamm, Germany; Magnet Theatre, Cape Town; National Arts Festival, Main Programme, Grahamstown.

Awards

Nominated for four Fleur Du Cap Awards 2015 (Best Actress, Best Solo Performance, Best New South African Script, Best Original Sound Design)
Nominated for two Naledi Awards 2017 (Best Cutting Edge Production, Best Original Score)

Produced by Magnet Theatre
Production copyright Magnet Theatre

magnet theatre

Reviews of the play

'Encapsulates masterful integration of layered narratives and character dimensions, visceral poetry.' —Malika Ndlovu

'*I turned away and she was gone* is by no means easy theatre, but it is rewarding. The delightful humour and the relevance of the production, anchored by the millennia of theatre that have come before it, makes this a play worth seeing.' —Izak de Vries, LitNet

'Magnificent ... a must.' —David Fick, *Broadway World*

'Takes the audience on a journey through emotions from anxiety to euphoria; it's relatable and taps into the deepest pools of our psyche.' —Megs Kelly, *Cue Media*

Notes for the play

We could therefore say that every mother contains her daughter in herself and every daughter her mother, and that every woman extends backwards into her mother and forwards into her daughter.

—Carl Jung

Three incarnations of women: a mother, a daughter and an old crone. A haunting of past, present and future selves. Drawing loosely on the Greek myth of Demeter and Persephone, this new solo play explores the process of individuation, the inevitability of the journey into the shadow and into the unknown, of the bonds that connect mothers and children to each other, of loss and the dense beautiful soaring life that we are all traveling through.

The central character of the narrator/actress transforms into all three women in the story: Demeter (the mother), Kore (the young girl), later to become Persephone, and Hecate (the old crone). There are shifts in voice and body that help indicate the changes in age and tone of the different women.

The play also makes use of an eclectic range of theatrical styles: Brechtian, Beckettian, story telling, Greek tragedy, clown, melodrama, dance, and physical theatre; unsettling the fixities of who we are and how we are represented. These styles integrate physical language, gesture with the dense poetic text, balance the present and ancient time, and make for a powerful visceral experience.

List of characters

Actress
Demeter
Kore, later to become Persephone
Hecate
All played by the same person

Set

Three-sided seating. Can also be performed front-on.
A rectangular floor painted white; grey at the edges
and grey 'shadows' around the objects. A small table
backstage centre with a smallish round metal bucket
filled with water on top of it. Underneath the table a
regular metal bucket with flowers, small towel, sheet
of newspaper and garden gloves. A central large oval
metal bath in the middle of the stage filled with water.
Stage right of the bath, a chair. A glass vase, stage
left and a metal jug. Another smaller metal vase with
'Missing' notices and a photograph inside it upstage
right. A dress hanging against the wall, or on a hatstand
backstage left. A microphone on a stand in front of
the hatstand back stage left on a grey-painted square.
Another empty oval bucket back stage right. A screen
at the back of the stage onto which the titles of each
section are projected.

Water Dripping.

The ACTRESS enters the stage. She places her water bottle next to one of the buckets and goes to hang up the towel she is carrying, looking up to the ceiling, trying to ascertain where the water is dripping from. She goes over to the glass vase and moves it slightly, to catch the imaginary drops. She looks over to the small bucket on the table and goes towards it. Looks at herself in the reflection of the water. Cups the water in her hands and watches it fall through the cracks. Starts to try and hold the water, catching it in her hands, but it always falls through. Suddenly, a storm brews in the bucket—she moves the water around vigorously and pulls out a bubble of water made from see-through plastic. She is surprised, uncomprehending. Holds the bubble delicately. Pats it. Slowly manoeuvres it over the edge of the bucket and onto the table. She gently moves the bubble across the table. The bubble seems to want to see over the edge. It peers over and gets a fright at the darkness over the edge. Pulls back. Sits; and then curiosity overcomes it and it (the bubble) looks over the front edge of the table. Pulls back in fear and then goes

forward to look again. Peering over the edge, it loses its balance,
fights to stay on the table and then falls onto the floor and bursts.
The ACTRESS reaches out in vain with an outstretched hand to
catch the bubble. Short, sharp intake of breath.

BLACKOUT

1. Demeter's Dream

[Title on screen]

ACTRESS:
The night before Persephone was born—but she wasn't called Persephone yet. In the beginning, she was called Kore. The night before Kore was born, her mother, Demeter, had this dream:

[Sits on the chair.]

DEMETER:
I am dreaming that I'm on holiday,
A tourist, I think, on this island.
Reunion Island, maybe.
And I drive to see this active volcano—driving across this desert,

A kind of moon-like, desolate landscape.

And I park the car in this parking lot

And then we climb and climb and climb to the top.

There is this zigzag path going all the way along the outside of the volcano to the very top.

And there you can look down and see into the

Dark hole.

[DEMETER falls in slow motion off the chair onto the floor and back up, exactly reversing the movement. Startled by the interruption, she continues.]

There is this place where the earth falls away rather abruptly and you can see into the deep, deep hole where the heart of the volcano is. There are no railings there, which is irresponsible really.

Anyway, I am standing there, looking over into the dark, when suddenly I lose my footing, the earth gives way or perhaps

I am pushed.

I start to slide down, feet first into the hole.

I have nothing and I am falling into the volcano.

I try to grab hold of the bushes and shrubs that are growing on the insides, but they uproot themselves and fall with me.

Again and again I clutch the air.

My feet scramble at emptiness.

My heart leaps into my throat.

And I am falling,

Falling and falling,

Faster and faster,

Just a heavy weight in the air.
Falling and falling and falling,
Infinitely,
Intolerably,
Into the dark.

[While she is saying this last line, she starts to slide slowly off the chair, an exaggerated, extended representation of falling. Stops on the word 'dark' spreadeagled on the floor. Pauses. And then as she starts talking, abruptly begins reversing the movement until she is sitting back on the chair.]

And then,
As I am falling, my body twisting and turning, hurtling down,
I start to look around me.
Whizzing past me I can just make out
The shape of trees—long, tall trunks of trees.
And I notice that they are quite beautiful, very tall and straight and full of leaves.
Perhaps it is spring.
And while I am falling,
I listen ...
[Faint sound of birds tweeting.]
Indistinct,
Distant,
Sporadic,
The sound of birds ... I can hear the faint sound of birds in this volcanic forest. Birdsong in this dense, beautiful, soaring forest that I am falling through.

[During the last sentence she falls again onto the floor. Tweeting fades.]

ACTRESS:

[Sitting up.] When she woke up, Demeter didn't remember her dream. Which perhaps is just as well.

BLACKOUT

2. The Garden

[Title on the screen]

During this section, the ACTRESS lays out newspaper, fetches flowers, separates them, puts on gloves—all the actions preparatory to putting flowers into a vase.

ACTRESS:

Demeter, Kore's mother, had made this garden. Well, not alone—with the help of her father. And Johannes. It was a substantial piece of land, about three-quarters of an acre overlooking the town, and in the distance, the Valley of a Thousand Hills. Kore had seen pictures of the 'before'. Rampant banana plants chopped back, weeds, wild grasses and unwanted trees, all cleared. The red earth exposed, chaotic, raw. Huge truckloads took away what they could and the rest was dumped at the bottom of the garden—where the steep hill dropped away. This was all before she was born.

It was an empty wound, a place for her mother to start again. *[Notices a cut on her finger from the 'flowers'. Fetches gloves to protect her hands. Puts them on.]* And then, now, the 'after', was sculptured, tailored, landscaped. There was lawn, rolling, lots of it; kikuyu I think, the tough insistent type. There were carefully manicured flowerbeds, bushes here, annuals there, shrubs by the gate, a huge mass of hydrangeas and a special, very special corner for her mother's roses. Icebergs—burgundy, white; Bella Rosas—bridal pink, red-gold, ruby-pearl, black magic, tea roses and floribundas. It was an intoxicating pathway. *[Arranges the flowers in the vase as she is speaking.]* Providing an endless flow of scent into the 'still lives', the vases her mother placed and replaced in the house. The layout was irreproachable; it was artful—secret benches and sundials, stone steps and overhangs. And her father's contribution, *[goes to fetch the bucket of water on the table]* as the hill gained momentum, of a curly, twisting water feature—a little stream really *[pauses to pour the water into a metal jug so that the sound of the water can be heard]*—that ran all the way down from the top of the hill. *[Filling the vase with water from the jug.]* The water flowed under little stone bridges, into baby ponds, miniature waterfalls and finally, into the chlorinated sky-blue pool. Machined, pumped, mechanically maintained by her father.

[Places the vase on the table.] And all of the rest, weeded (ruthlessly), cut, filed, manured, watered, sluggemed, daily, by her mother. And Johannes. *[Cleaning up.]* Demeter had made this garden paradise for her daughter. *[With a towel, she wipes up the water that was spilt on the floor when the bubble burst.]* It was her life's work and she had made it for Kore. And for a long while they were both very, very happy there. Content. Complete.

BLACKOUT

3. The things they loved about each other

[Title on screen]

*This section is worked with a physical language based on the
'hand gym' that mothers do endlessly around babies and
children: the holding, tucking, letting go, rocking, massaging,
etc., and which they repeat when caring for older parents. It
is interspersed during and in-between the text. 'Tutting' is
also used as an inspiration for the style of movement. Music
underscores this section.*

ACTRESS:

These are the things that the mother, Demeter and the
young daughter, Kore loved about each other:

Her unbearable beauty
The stranger in her green eyes

The reassuring bite of her perfume
The silken slide of her cheek
Her cerise-tipped fingers
Her tiny hands
The memory of chlorine on her skin
Her unbearable beauty.

Her sudden laughter when she reads something funny
The sound of her keys around her neck
The blood colour of her lips
Her Raphaelite hair.

When she tells stories of when she was a baby
When she tell stories of when I was a baby
Her demanding companionship
Her angular presence in the house
Her voice when she speaks her mind.

When I feel her ears fill up with my secrets
When I feel her listening body soften
When she is there
When she arrived
When she sends me running to the post-box to fetch
the letters
When she comes home with the weight of school on
her back
When she comes home
When she opens her arms
When she unlocks the door.

That she weeps when the story gets sad
Ignores the mess in her cupboards
That she pushes aside the furniture in the lounge
in order to dance and dance
The way she insists I listen and watch
How she makes me her prisoner.

Her meticulous schedules
Her hand-written shopping lists
Her torn fingernails
Her hair turning to grey
Her surreptitious beauty spots
Her laughing crow's feet
Her unbearable beauty.

Watching illegally downloaded movies with her,
huddled around her laptop
Admiring her compose cut-flower extravaganzas
Watching her hair turn
How she mourned her father
How she talks to babies
Her hungry attention
Her animated liveliness
Her gaze
Her regard
Her look
Her unbearable beauty.

Music fades.

Girl Dance: Sequence to Neo Muyanga's version of 'It's wonderful'—an expression, initially, of the playfulness and freedom of a young girl. Moments of release, joy. Language developed from childhood games of elastic and hopscotch. As the dance progresses, the girl experiences moments of 'stuckness' that get progressively more and more difficult for her to release from. Her hips also start to misbehave and begin a continuous circular movement that she cannot control. The continually moving hips and the 'stuckness' intensify until she collapses on the floor.

ACTRESS:

[Same physical language from 'The things they loved about each other' but transposed into gestures made on the floor as if she were playing an imaginary game during the following text.]

In her mother's house Kore's body remained flat, secretive, like a desert. Smooth. Shiny. Angular. She was trying to think while the polisher hummed and hummed and hummed, punishing the impeccable parquet. The parquet ran throughout the house. Little rectangular pieces of wood fitting comfortably together, shining now and reflecting: her flat-chested, boney, imbalanced ugliness, before the face settles into something.

KORE:

Who am I?

What can I be?

Am I outside my mother's body?

If I was once inside, or still am, is it safe?

Can I breathe?

What can I do? Where can I go? What can I be?

ACTRESS:
The floors were very quiet.
Yet she could hear something,
Something breathing.

BLACKOUT

4. The Wild

[Title on the screen]

Stuck to the floor trying to get free to reach the end of the garden.

ACTRESS:
At the bottom of the garden, at the very, very bottom, where the steep hill dropped away, past the extremely mown lawn and the delicately tended icebergs and floribundas, and the careful architecture of the water feature, was the wild. Barely kept at bay by a low, rusty barbed-wire fence in need of repair—The Wild. Breathing.
A place that came with her mother's strictest warning: Don't. Ever.
[She moves towards the central bath.]
A pool of water, not domesticated like this.
But dark and invisible. Deep.
[Noticing her reflection in the water.]
Her skin smooth
Her lips red
Her Raphaelite hair, longer, much longer than this.
Her eyes,
Incandescent, unblemished.
A square trunk hinting at a softer spread
Her angles anticipating crescents.

Music throughout next sections, until she collapses in the bath: strings tugging, pulling, repetitive and emotional. Sequence of falling in love with her own reflection in the water in the

*bucket. Movements are quite sensual, of discovery, a tango
feel in the lower body. She moves first around the bucket.
Then she feels embarrassed by the sensuality that has been
released and walks away, ashamed. She is drawn back,
however, to the water. As she speaks the next text, there is a
sequence on the floor, slightly animalistic.*

KORE:

Is that who I am? Is that what I can be?
I am sooo thirsty; so, so thirsty,
Thirsty for something I can't even name
Thirsty for somewhere I don't even know
For someone, something, somewhere, somehow
So, so thirsty ...

LIGHTS CHANGE. MUSIC CONTINUES

5. Regret at having left too soon, or fear perhaps

[Title on the screen]

She runs to the wall, frantic that she can't get back to the house, that there is a wall between her and home. Sequence of pushing against the wall, using the same physical language as the language around the bucket, but this time up against the wall, frantic and desperate to get away from the water.

KORE:
Cut down!
Clear away!
Pull out the weeds, fell the trees!
What monster is this?
What monster?

ACTRESS:
[She turns slowly around, movements fading.]
But birds had eaten the crumbs,
Lifted the stone path,
And the way back was barred.
[Leaning against the wall, writing her name with her foot in the sand.]
She was a good girl
She carved her name in the bark of her mother's tree
Leaving her girl's name behind
Kore
Kore
Leaving it behind.

BLACKOUT
MUSIC CONTINUES, BUILDING

6. Kore going

[Title on the screen]

During this sequence, KORE goes into the water in the central bucket. This is a sequence that starts slowly, full of release and relief and breath that becomes more and more intense and hungry as it progresses. The physical language is based on gestures that involve washing the body—wiping, soaping, rubbing and drying. The gestures are extended and developed into a choreographic sequence.

ACTRESS:

Music.

She could hear music

Coming from the underneath of the water.

From the other side

From the dark *[steps into the water]*

Out of the deep.

An in-and-out
A swell of ribs
A rhythm.
A collapse, a bursting, a waiting and then again
Insisting.
Wild breath, in and out, on and on,
Beating and beating and beating.

[Sequence develops slowly and then stops as she speaks.]

I don't think she even looked back at her mother who
was for a moment looking away. I don't think she
even saw her standing there at the top of the lawn
untangling the hose pipe, spraying the air, watering the
weeds.

Her thirst ungovernable and utterly irresistible.

See how she is dancing.
She is dancing at the door.
You can't dance that hard without
Something happening,
Something shifting,
Something opening.
*[Now the dance develops an urgency and hunger that is almost
akin to drowning. Climaxes with ...]*
Beating and beating and beating ...

SLOW FADE TO BLACKOUT. MUSIC FADES

LIGHTS UP

The ACTRESS is collapsed in the bath, breathing heavily from the exertion of the previous sequence. The lights come up brightly, including the audience, as if the show is over. She pants, exhausted. She talks directly to the audience.

ACTRESS:

You know, one thing that I have understood about growing older: it's not that you can't do things ... you can ... you just have to build in recovery periods.

[Addressing someone in the audience.] Please, man, sorry. Won't you just bring me my water bottle? Thank you so much ... such service ...

[Opens bottle to drink.] I won't be a minute, just read your programme ... talk amongst yourselves ... *[drinks]* I have to wait for my heart rate to return to normal ...

Okay, Tarryn, *[addressing the stage manager]* I'm almost there ...

[Thumbs up, but lights don't immediately change—irritated and insisting, she indicates again and the lights change.]

LIGHTS CHANGE

7. The river

[Title on the screen]

KORE:

Where am I?

What place is this?

How did I get here?

Who am I?

My name is Kore.

My mother had a garden.

Has a garden?

What is this water?

This very dark muddied water

That I am floating in?

I remember the sound of music. Wild music.

I was at the centre, at the origin of the music. My beat,

its beat. Measured exactly. And then at the precise moment when we lined up completely—the beat and me—I lost my balance, or perhaps I was pushed and fell. Bum first. Hands, feet, arms flailing at the darkness.

That's what I remember ...

My name is Kore

My mother is ...

Where is this boat taking me?

To the other side?

Is there another side?

How black and silky the water is.

How dark.

How silent.

I am thinking that I know who I am

But my body is a stranger

Unfamiliar and contemporary

Without an echo of a previous time.

Where is she?

That previous one

That was/*is* me?

Where did I leave her?

Did I misplace her?

Did she slip away?

Crafty and without warning?

My name is ...

What is my name?

I know I had a name

Given to me by my mother.

I know I had a mother

What is her name?

I think I remember her eyes

Green, yes green

Or were they big black pools?

This water is tugging at me, tugging and pulling and towing

Deeper and faster now

Away further and further away.

Eyes, a faint trace of a smell, a familiar ...

Wait!

Wait!

A secret bench, cerise-tipped fingernails, a polisher?

Wait!

I think I am drowning,

The ink is over my head

My name ...

My ...

I cannot

I cannot recall

I cannot retrieve

I cannot review, cannot revert

P... M ... T ... S ... F ... J ...

What is my name?

This place ...? This river?

I am going,

Going

Going

Gone.

BLACKOUT

8. Underworld?

[Title on screen]

ACTRESS goes to a microphone at the right back of the stage and addresses the audience directly. Drone sound underscoring following text.

ACTRESS:

Okay. This is the black hole at the centre of the piece. Where has Kore gone? What is the Underworld and how do we represent it?

[Takes off dress and reaches for towel and begins to dry herself. Returns to the microphone.] Is the Underworld her unconscious, her rich dark space, her shadow? Or is it that terrifying dark space where we understand suffering and, through opposition, learn how to live?

[Leans down to dry off her legs and feet away from the microphone, but continues to speak into it when she apologises for the interruption.] Sorry ... And then, how do we represent this unconscious? With light and sound? Hey, Craig? *[Addressing the designer.]* Maybe. I don't know. *[Reaches for another dress hanging on the wall and puts it on while talking.]* I think there needs to be a series of rivers ... a river of woe, a river of fire—the river Styx. The river of unbreakable oaths and the river of forgetfulness. That memory flush that happens at adolescence that washes away early childhood memories ...

BLACKOUT

9. A moment ago

[Title on screen]

DEMETER:
Kore?
Kore?

[Addressing the audience.] Have you seen my daughter? She was here a moment ago. Have you seen her?

Here
Not here
Here
Not here!
Kore?
Gone?

My girl
My daughter
My young
My youth
Here
A moment ago
Just a moment.

She has been taken
My girl
My daughter
My young
My youth
A moment ago
Just a moment.
I looked away for a moment
Busied myself with something else for a moment
I turned away
And she was taken.

There is no air in this house!
Stop. Stop time.
Stop moving me away from the moment when she was
here standing in front of me, looking into my eyes.
Stop dragging me from that moment.
It was just a moment ago she was here
And she was my baby
And I did all those things a mother does
A moment ago
For all those years.

[Showing an old photograph of the ACTRESS's mother as a young girl to the audience.]

Have you seen my girl?
Look closely!
Have you seen her?
Please?
Someone similar in the street?
Crossing the road, in the supermarket, on a bus, in a taxi perhaps?

[Distributing 'Missing' posters with an image of a contemporary girl, perhaps the ACTRESS herself, when she was younger.]

Look at her clothes
They are all she had with her
Perhaps you recognise something
Perhaps you remember something
Someone similar perhaps.
She has that long Raphaelite hair
Unbearably beautiful
A little unusual I think
And an infectious laugh
Although perhaps she isn't laughing now.

[Drops 'Missing' poster on the floor. Goes to the round bucket of water. Ritualised gestures based on the language of the 'hand gym' from the beginning.]

I did all those things:

Holding, feeding, brushing, tucking, smoothing,
rocking, leading, talking, listening, lifting, spreading,
cooking, offering, healing, pouring, sticking, washing,
rubbing, drying, making, bullying, giving,

And for a moment I looked away.

Not here.

What hell has she been taken to?

[Moves around the stage.] Stop the heave-and-fill. The
in-and-out. The swell of ribs. Suck out the air.

Stop. Stop time.

Stop the cells from multiplying, the leaves from uncurling,
the roots from deepening, the stream from flowing.

Stop the breath exchanging, the ties binding, the
promises keeping.

Stop it all!

Stop the fruits from ripening,

The tap from dripping,

The fire from burning,

The ash from smoking!

[Tears the flowers out of the vase and throws them on the floor.
Pours the water from the vase over her head—sharp intake of
breath in shock.]

And let there be
An absence.

Her absence.
Only.
Emptiness.
Only.
A stopping.
Only.

[Places the vase upside down on the stage, trapping the emptiness. Picks up one of the 'Missing' posters and starts to fold it into an origami boat during the next text.]

She will not remember me;
Time will pass and she will not remember me.
She will not remember my name.
She will forget my green eyes, my cerise-tipped fingers.
Forget the hands that wrapped and soothed.
She will forget the sound of my voice
The mess in my cupboards,
My hair turning to grey.
Time will pass and she will forget.
When I pass her on the street she will not recognise me
She will slide past without a second glance
And I, rooted to the spot—
My gaze
My look
My regard, following her back as she pushes past.
Time will pass and I will pass.
And she will remember nothing.

[Places paper boat in the central bath and watches it float for a moment. Returns to the microphone. Taps it.]

Thank you. Please, I am appealing to you. If you can hear this broadcast. If you have taken my daughter. Please do not hurt her. Please. Before it's too late. Please. If you can hear me. Give me back my daughter. Bring her back to me. I won't do anything. I will not press charges. You can just walk away. Just. Bring. Her. Back. To. Me!

BLACKOUT

10. What the old woman Hecate saw and which no one believed

[Title on screen]

HECATE:

I can manage perfectly well on my own thank you, Demeter.

[Manoeuvres herself to get into the bath. Toe in.]

Aargh! *[Quickly withdraws her foot.]*

It is as hot as hell! I am not dead yet.

I said it's too hot.

No one ever believes a word I say.

[Watches DEMETER pour in cold water. Tests it and slowly releases herself into the water. Under her breath muttering, 'that's better, that's lovely'.]

She has put out the light.

She has put out the light.

You thought it was Eskom.

Mad. Stark, raving.

Not me, Hecate.

She. Her.

Demeter.

Stark, raving mad.

You have no idea what is going on here. You have no idea what I am living with. What she is putting me through.

A darkness before its dark.

My throat is choking on the dust.

Her own private scorched-earth policy

And we have not withdrawn

We are stuck here

She and I.

And nothing,

Nothing grows,

Nothing moves—

Not the bushes, not the shrubs, not the hydrangeas by the gate—

Nothing slips even slightly.

We are in hell

Kore. Or whatever it is you call yourself these days.

Your mother has gone mad.

She has left the building

And turned off the lights.

[Washing herself, using the same language as KORE used in the water, but transposed onto her older body and sitting in the bucket.]

You fear, Demeter
That she was taken,
Pulled away by some rough-handed man,
Hard-bodied and unmovable
Like steel,
Gun or whip or knife or rope at her throat.
That is what you fear. *[Stops washing. Notices the soap.]*
Demeter,
Pass me the ... linen, the bed, the fur, the penis, the can opener
The soap! I mean the soap!
I've lost the word.

Not because I forget, but because it doesn't matter anymore.

You fear, Demeter that she was taken
Like some are.
I see them—
Many others:
A young girl walking in the street
Forced into a car, a taxi.
On her way home in-between one place and another
Unanchored
In-between.

Primed to be taken
Too light to scream loudly for anyone except me to hear.
Easy prey
To the traders, the war mongers, the flesh dealers.
I see the gap in the street
The displaced sand that settles
Around the memory of the girl
A moment ago
Standing on the sidewalk.

No need to know the word for ... vacuum cleaner, nipple,
washing powder, bowel ...
Soap.

But they don't speak to me
Don't interview me.
Don't listen when I say
I saw her. She was wearing such and such.
I saw the car. It was a dark blue Corsa.
I saw the man; there is always a man
A man out the corner of your eye
Following, waiting, rushing up, surprising.
I recognised him. I saw the car door open
I saw the yank and her dancing feet
Trying for purchase on the pavement.
I didn't get the ... *[tries to indicate what she means—the
number plate]*.
Never mind, next time.
But they ignore me.
No one acts

No one does anything.

Over and over they go.

They disappear, they vanish, they evaporate, vacate the warm space of their being, their young remnants found

Sometimes

Somewhere else.

Their pieces

Never reconfigured as the girl they once were on the pavement.

And I see it. I see it all, in all directions

Here at the crossroads.

Every sale, every coercion, every whispered promise.

Every hard crack and dismemberment.

And there is always a man!

And I always tell.

And they never listen.

Why doesn't anyone act?

Why are you all still sitting here? *[Addressing the audience.]*

There, on the main road, in that subway, on that empty field!

Listening but not understanding.

Outside that restaurant, in your home, in your school, in your village, in the theatre!

Get up! *Get up*!

I keep telling and I keep saying and I keep revealing.

Get up! Get up!

Nothing. Filed away

'We are addressing the increase in ...

It is of great concern to us that ...'

It is a war!

Where is the army?
Oh yes, I remember,
Outside parliament.
There goes another *[clicks fingers]*
And another *[click]*
And another *[click]*
Our girls, going, going, gone. *[Click.]*
And no one listens to me
Because they say I can't remember the name for bone,
throat, slip, buttocks, soap.

Many of them go that way. The girls. Too soon and too
completely.

[DEMETER pours some more hot water into the bath.]

Aaargh. Thank you. A top-up!
But not your Kore.
She cried out in pleasure.

You don't believe me, you say.
I know.
That she could have wanted to leave your paradise,
ached to disappear into the dark of the garden never to
return.
Longed to be free of you,
Your prisoner.
Well Kore's gone.
Her feet walked their own way down there.
How lovely to be able to blame

Another.

Better than to hear that she cried out, not in fear, but in desperation to be free.

I am telling the truth.

I was there.

I heard her.

'Free, ah free, free ...' *[She mocks.]*

You say I am cruel.

How cruel your disappearing of me

When I am still here.

Still breathing.

Yes, that's me. That still in and out of my breath

That awful sound.

I hear you whispering beyond my door, carving up the year so I might be parcelled off between the four of you.

A seasonal rotation.

I hear you debating the cost of assisted dying,

Of medical insurances and living wills,

Circling past my bed as if I am not in it.

Cruel, you say?

I was glorious once

Until you reconfigured me as this old hag,

Biddy

Crone

Wrinkly

Old bat, bag.

Witch.

Has-been.

I was Hecate, goddess of the moon;

Earth, sky and sea my kingdoms.

Walking in the street—

Graciously, effortlessly magnetising the gaze of men
(and women)

My momentary hostages.

Now I have no disciples.

I am the dark grey crack in the pavement.

Pass the soap!

BLACKOUT

11. By the river bank

[Title on screen]

KORE picks up the fallen flowers. During the text she lays them around the upside-down vase as if laying them around a grave.

KORE:
Someone died.
I will dig a grave
Small
For the smallest kind of body;
Shallow
So she can just touch life a little,
Reach up and touch
Next to the river;
This river I have crossed

Floated
So she can hear the sound of rain.
I will say a prayer
Sing it
So she can hear the sound of laughter.
I will pat the earth over her
Gently so the warmth fills her ears and mouth.
I will say goodbye
I will turn away.
I will forget her name
Kore
Her child's name.

And I will construct another:
Persephone.

BLACKOUT

12. Demeter's search

[Title on screen]

While the ACTRESS talks, she creates an image of running which is stylised, on the spot, fast, lifting her legs in a running motion, with her arms supporting her weight on the table. It is exhausting.

ACTRESS:

So Demeter searches the world for her daughter— firstly in those places where she thinks she may have been taken. Brothels and known trafficking sites. She visits hospitals and morgues. Pores over police files and unidentified bodies. *[Moves around the stage.]* And then reluctantly, she starts to search in those places where Kore may have gone of her own free will. Beaches, islands, New York City, the theatre.

Sometimes she hears strange bits of news.
That she has taken another name,
Discarded her own.
The years pass and Demeter waits.
Not a text. Not a WhatsApp?
Not even an email.

[She repeats the falling sequence in DEMETER's dream—from the table to the floor and back up again.]

She behaves like a mad woman and people keep their distance.
She makes strangers her confidante:

[Goes up close and personal to an audience member, moving and sitting on a chair next to them. Repeats the same falling sequence as in DEMETER's dream at the beginning of the play again.]

DEMETER:
My daughter
She has broken my heart.
I cannot go back and undo the mess that I have made
I cannot tidy up
Unburn the garden.
She left.
[To another audience member.]
I thought she was taken, as some others are.
I thought I could weep like some other mothers for their daughters who are stolen, uncovered in shallow graves, but, no.

She

Left

Me.

[Advances on another audience member.]

So now I wait for some scrap of news.

Something to occupy my plate.

Wait for that little red light to flash

(Yes, I've got one of those old Blackberries ...)

For me to read:

Hello Mom, it's me, it's Kore. Sorry for all the worry

Or

Please forgive me

Or, I have not forgotten

Or just

I am ...

BLACKOUT

13. Persephone's Dream

[Title on screen]

ACTRESS:
The night before Persephone left the Underworld to return to her mother she had this dream.

PERSEPHONE:
[Sitting in a chair. Interspersing following text with physical language of washing, wiping, wringing out, unlocking; working also with breath.]
I dream that I am standing next to an open grave.
It is open but not empty.
I think it is a grave or perhaps just a hole in the ground.
I can dimly see the form of something, someone under the earth at the bottom of the hole.
A lump.

The earth around is agitated, churned up as if someone
has been digging around and around.

Turning the earth over and over

Red

Dark

Raw

The earth is dark red.

It reminds me of the colour of the earth in KwaZulu.

From my home.

My knees are stinging. I look down and they are grazed
and covered in mud, my bare feet, too. My hands and up
to my elbows are stained by dark red mud.

It dawns on me that this turbulent, agitated spot is of
my own making. That I had scrambled around in the
dirt,

On my knees,

Digging and

Digging.

Digging for something.

For someone.

That it is *my* fault.

I swat at my grazed knees, trying to brush the loose soil
off. Spit. Rub. Wipe. Brush. Spit. Rub. Wipe. Brush.

But the stain remains.

ACTRESS:

When Persephone woke up she didn't remember her
dream. Which perhaps is just as well.

BLACKOUT

14. What Demeter says to her daughter when she at last opens the door to find it is Persephone who has knocked

[Title on screen]

Knocking on the table as if someone is knocking at the door.

DEMETER:
You say you are Persephone,
My daughter Persephone?
I do not have a daughter called Persephone.
What kind of name is that?
My daughter's name is Kore.
Kore.

[Turns away and knocks again.]

You were she?
I don't think so.
She did not look like you.
Not like you at all.
You say it was a long time ago.
I don't think so.
Here, in this house, time stood still
Waiting for her return.
Hers not yours.
For you are an imposter, I think.
After an inheritance
A titbit from my table.
You say 'Look at me;
Don't you recognise me?'
I am looking—
Where is your long Raphaelite hair
Your young girl's laugh when you read something funny,
Your never-ending secrets
Your demanding companionship
Your silken cheeks
Your look
Your black eyes?
You are nothing like my daughter.
'Mother', you call me.
I don't think so.

[Turns her back on her daughter and the knocking comes again, more insistent.]

What have you done with her?
My girl
My daughter
My young
My youth
My Kore?
What heavy adult has stolen her name
And faint echo of her hair?
And what have you done to her hands? They are red,
Stained.
What have you done?
What crime are you guilty of?
Wait there. Don't move.

[Goes to microphone.]

Tell me—
This is a test:
One two, one two, *[tapping the microphone]*
A security check—
What are the things we loved about each other?

LIGHTS CHANGE

15. What Persephone has done, whilst she was gone

[Title on screen]

Climbing onto the table, PERSEPHONE tries to remember the gestures from 'The things they loved about each other'; with difficulty at the beginning, and then gaining in clarity as she is talking.

PERSEPHONE:
I rode on a motor bike
I skied in the Canadian Rockies
I flew an aeroplane
I loved a man
I breathed.
I wrote a poem (in fact, a whole play)
I loved a woman
I carried a child
And gave birth to another
I planted a garden
I lived in the night
I counted the stars
I breathed.
I read a map
I got lost
I was found
I followed a trail
I tamed a wolf
I fell into a volcano
I dressed as a man

I healed a bird
I danced and danced
I swam in a bottomless pool.
I was afraid.
I was unafraid.
I breathed.
I went to Antarctica
I stayed at home
I cooked a meal
I polished the glass
I loved a baby
And I loved a child
I said goodbye
And I breathed.
I ate sushi and snails and North Indian curry
I was thirsty and I drank
I was wounded and bled
I was quiet.
And I listened.
I tasted the juice of a strange hard-shelled fruit
Crushed the bloody baubles
And the colour of it stained my lips.
Shall I go on?

ACTRESS:
[Climbing off the table.] Demeter, older now, replies:

DEMETER:
You are rude

Cruel, to come back here like this
With your stranger's name.
Now, to wash me and lift me and carry me and change me
To listen to my noisy breath
And then to go again.
Ah, and so you do.
You have your own life now
Persephone
As I have heard,
And how well it suits you. Your wonderful life
Your own home and adventures
Your career, your children
Your loving husband whom you cannot live without.
How beautiful he is, you say. Unbearably.
And your children. Unbearably beautiful.
A boy and a girl you say? Good luck.
Good luck to you when time clutches at your heart so
you can no longer breathe
Or say their names for the pain they have caused you.
Today, I think I will die *today*!
Definitely, today.
Look how short my breath is, how rasping, how sparse.
But no, still you pack your bags,
The short visit over.
And I have to wait the whole winter through to see you
again
My beloved daughter.
I don't think I will last, I say, begging
Don't go.
Don't leave.

My beloved.

See how the light is fading ...

Keep the door open just a little.

My daughter.

ACTRESS:

[Packs all the buckets and the chair onto the table except the big bucket in the middle and the vase and flowers.]

Summer faded when Persephone left. If she was well, Demeter collected the fallen leaves and warmed herself next to a winter fire, her back to the cold, closing her eyes until the hint of spring and her daughter's return. As for summers ... there were to be few in number.

BLACKOUT

16. The terrible, terrible noise

[Title on screen]

Lying in the water in the central bucket. Breathing loudly. Same gestures as in PERSEPHONE's dream but transposed onto a much older body.

HECATE OR DEMETER OR KORE:
What is that noise?
What is that terrible, terrible noise?
Oh my God
I think it's me
I think it's me.
No wonder they can't wait for it to be over.
What a god-awful noise.
Good heavens

[She sniffs something bad]

And that smell?
Surely ...
Oh God. Not ...
Yes.
Mea culpa.
It's me.
I think it must be me.
Please.
Who are all these strangers?
Anxious faces gathered round the bed.
A woman—that must be my daughter
I am sure I had a daughter ... and who's that with her?
Handsome devil. I didn't have a son.
I don't think ...
A husband. Not mine. *Hers.* Mine is long gone.
Her husband.
Did she have to bring him in here?
And those others?
Could they be my grandchildren?
Green hair and Raphaelite eyes ...
What are they doing here?
Looking so anxious.
I am not sure children should be exposed to this.
I don't think it's appropriate.
Waiting for the next breath ...

[Noisily draws in her breath, waits ... does not exhale.]

Was that the last?

Is that it?

Come on, don't disappoint.

Just squeeze out another.

Come on, swing those ribs,

Suck in the air.

Come on, come on

Just one more

Look

Look how they are waiting.

These four strangers.

[Exhales. Sucks in another breath.]

Ahh ...

That was close.

She who calls me 'mother' has divided up the jewellery

And what's left of the annuities—

Not much, and even put the house on the market.

She didn't waste much time,

But at least it is spring

And they are here

And you are here

At a safe distance

All gathered for the final moment.

'Mother' ...

I don't think that is my name.

I think it was something else.

I can't remember now but it had a different ring to it,

I am sure.

My name ...

I saw it once

Growing in a tree

A name

My name

My name perhaps

Not 'Mother'

No.

See, see there it is, in the bark,

Carved

Kore ...

Perhaps that is my name

Kore.

Yes, I seem to remember something like that.

Oh God, now she is crying.

Big heavy sobs

Ugly contorted face, blotchy eyes and nose

Chunking and heaving

A waterfall;

What a fuss

Blubbering into his white shirt.

[Laughing.] I don't think those mascara stains will wash out.

You would think someone has died.

[Suddenly stops laughing, slow realisation.]

Have I?

Already?

Did I go without me noticing?

Did I slip away while I was thinking of something else?

Was I pushed? *[Breathes last breath in and out.]*

LIGHTS FADE

Sound of birds. Repeat of Neo Muyanga's version of 'It's wonderful'. Video image of a young girl bouncing up and down in slow motion in a forest of trees projected onto the screen. The ACTRESS gets out of the bath. Fetches her towel, tenderly and warmly looking at the image of the young girl. Fetches her water bottle—focus still on the image. Exits stage. Music continues to play.

BLACKOUT

THE END

Acknowledgements

Mark Fleishman, partner, friend and co-creator—our love, work and family are richly woven together and I am profoundly grateful for who you are and what we have made together. Hannah-Rose and Zac who let me use the details of our lives together in my creative life and who gave me cause. Craig Leo, Neo Muyanga, Ina Wichterich and Sanjin Muftić for their visual, aural and physical forms (respectively) that all helped to contain the journey. Magnet Theatre and all who work and play under its roof for their dedication and support and space. The University of Cape Town who offered me an empty room when Magnet was overflowing. Jacques Lecoq—grand maître—who gave me the gift of myself. Other wordsmiths who inspired me to fashion my own: Gabeba Baderoon, Julia Martin, Malika Ndlovu. Modjaji for agreeing to publish and offering the adventure and challenge of translating the body in performance into text. The communion of mothers, daughters and grandmothers who witnessed the work and allowed it to speak to their own histories of growing older, of loss, grief and transformation.

About Magnet Theatre

Magnet Theatre is based in Cape Town and has been at the forefront of the South African theatre industry for 31 years, creating groundbreaking educational programmes and award-winning productions that have toured to acclaim nationally and across four continents and in over 30 international festivals. Their longest running show *Every year every day I am walking* has been published by Junkets in *Collected Series No.4 The Magnet Theatre 'Migration' Plays*. They have created a crucial space for theatre, education, performance and community, always in response to South Africa, its context and history. Alongside their profile of professional theatre productions, they have pioneered performance for early years audiences and produced the first ever South African play for mothers and babies under the age of 12 months. They run a multilayered structure of youth development programmes including the Farm Schools and Culture Gangs Programmes (creating gangs of youth committed to culture and not to crime), The Fulltime Training and Job Creation Programme (bridging from township schools to university and employment) and various internship programmes. The impact of the company is documented in the book *Magnet Theatre: Three decades of making space*, edited by Anton Krueger and Megan Lewis and recently published by Intellect.

About Jennie Reznek

BA, Perf. Dip. (Speech & Drama, UCT), Diploma Ecole Jacques Lecoq (Paris), MA (UCT). Actress, director and teacher, Jennie is a founder member of Magnet Theatre in Cape Town. She runs the bulk of the youth development and performance programme of the company along with co-artistic directors Mark Fleishman and Mandla Mbothwe, and is an award-winning actress. She has created 27 new pieces of physical theatre under the banner of Magnet Theatre which foreground the language of the body and respond to the South African archive, most notably the multi-award-winning *The show's not over til the fat lady sings* and *Every year every day I am walking* which has garnered praise and awards both nationally and internationally and has been performed in 17 countries all over the world. She has recently been responsible for developing work specifically for audiences under the age of seven and has developed eight new works that have toured nationally and internationally. *I turned away and she was gone* is her latest solo show and has been nominated for six awards.

Printed in the United States
By Bookmasters